Der Wackelzahn

The Wibbly Wobbly Tooth

Written by David Mills
Illustrated by Julia Crouth

German translation by Nick Barkow

mantra

Am Montag Abend um zwei Minuten nach sieben entdeckte Li seinen ersten Wackelzahn.
Der Zahn wackelte hin und wackelte her.

On Monday evening at two minutes past seven, Li got his first wobbly tooth.
And the tooth went...Wibble Wobble.

THIS BOOK BELONGS TO:

_____

_____

_____

mantra

For the children of Richard Cobden Primary School, London
D.M.

Special thanks to Phillip Fong and his family,
and to the staff and children of Mason Avenue Kindergarten
J.C.

First published 2003 by Mantra
5 Alexandra Grove, London N12 8NU
www.mantralingua.com

Text copyright © 2003 David Mills
Illustrations copyright © 2003 Julia Crouth
Dual language copyright © 2003 Mantra

British Library Cataloguing in Publication Data:
a catalogue record for this book is available
from the British Library.

On Tuesday, he had to show everyone at school.
And the tooth went...Wibble Wobble.

Am Dienstag musste er ihn jedem in der Schule zeigen,
und der Zahn wackelte hin und wackelte her.

Am Mittwoch musste er beim Essen sehr vorsichtig sein, denn der Zahn wackelte hin und wackelte her.

On Wednesday, he had to be careful eating his lunch.
And the tooth went...Wibble Wobble, Wibble Wobble.

Am Donnerstag musste er beim Zähneputzen furchtbar vorsichtig sein,
denn der Zahn wackelte hin und wackelte her.

On Thursday, Li had to be extremely careful brushing his teeth.
And the tooth went...Wibble Wobble, Wibble Wobble, Wibble.

Am Freitag liess Li seinen
Zahn vor- und zurückwackeln,

On Friday, Li wiggled his tooth in
and out,

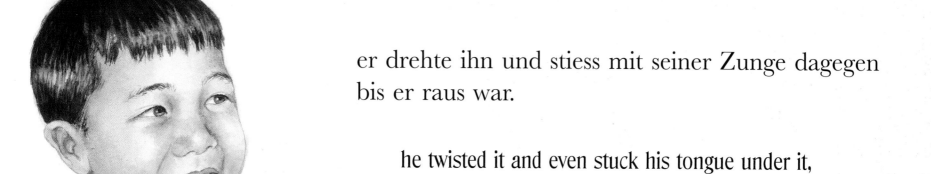

er drehte ihn und stiess mit seiner Zunge dagegen
bis er raus war.

he twisted it and even stuck his tongue under it,
until it went...

HIN, HER, HIN, HER,
HIN, HER...

HOPPLA!

WIBBLE WOBBLE, WIBBLE
WOBBLE,
WIBBLE WOBBLE...

OOOOPS!

"HURRAY!" everyone cheered.
Li gave them a big smile and he felt very brave.

Alle riefen "Hurrah!"
Li strahlte über das ganze Gesicht und hatte das Gefühl von Tapferkeit.

Als in der Schule Schluss war lief Li gleich heim um es dem Papa zu zeigen.

When it was time to go home, Li rushed out to show his dad.

"Endlich," sagte Papa,
"gut gemacht!"

"At last," said Dad.
"Well done!"

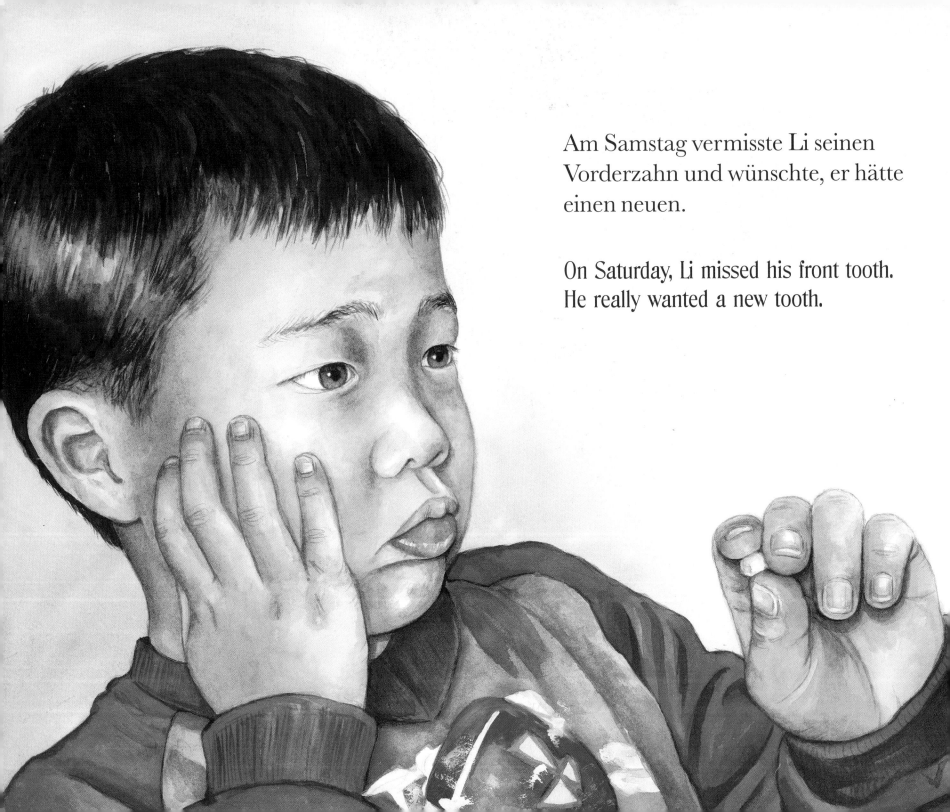

Am Samstag vermisste Li seinen
Vorderzahn und wünschte, er hätte
einen neuen.

On Saturday, Li missed his front tooth.
He really wanted a new tooth.

"Na los," sagte Papa, "Gehen wir die Grossmutter besuchen,
die wird schon wissen was man machen kann."
So gingen sie zur Grossmutter.

"Come on," said Dad, "let's go and see Grandma. She'll know just what to do."
So off they went to Grandma's.

"Guck mal," sagte Li.
"Hey, du hast deinen Zahn verloren," sagte Joey. "Wen du ihn unter dein Kopfkissen legst wird die Zahnfee kommen, und dir Geld bringen!"
"Warum?" fragte Li.
"Sie braucht deinen Zahn um ihr neues Haus zu bauen!"
"Oh," sagte Li, "das muss ich gleich meiner Grossmutter erzählen."

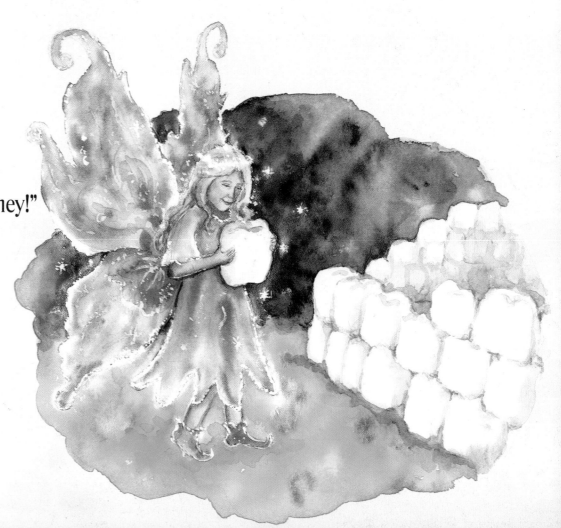

"Look!" said Li.
"Hey, you've lost your tooth!" said Joey.
"If you put it under the pillow, the tooth fairy will come and bring you some money!"
"Why?" asked Li.
"She needs your tooth to build her new house!"
"Oh," said Li. "I'd better tell my Grandma!"

"Guck mal!" sagte Li.
"Oooooo!" sagte Kofi. "Ich habe meinen im Boden vergraben und dann wuchs mir ein neuer Zahn."
"Wirklich?" fragte Li. "Das muss ich meiner Grossmutter erzählen!"

"Look!" said Li.
"Oooooo!" said Kofi. "I hid mine in the ground and then my new one grew!"
"Did it really? I must tell my Grandma!"

"Guck mal," sagte Li.
"Hey," sagte Salma. "Wenn du deinen Zahn in den Fluss wirfst wird dir das Glück bringen."
"Wirklich?" fragte Li. "Was soll ich machen Papa?"
"Die Grossmutter wird das schon wissen," sagte Papa.

"Look!" said Li.
"Hey," said Salma. "You could throw your tooth into the river and it will bring you good luck!"
"It will?" said Li. "Dad, what shall I do?"
"Grandma knows," said Dad.

"Oma, Oma guck mal," sagte Li. "Mein Zahn wackelte hin und her, hin und her - und draussen war er!"
"Na sowas," freute sich die Grossmutter. "Ich weiss auch was du jetzt damit tun musst," flüsterte sie. "Wirf ihn auf das Dach des Nachbarn und denk dir einen grossen Wunsch."
"Okay," rief Li und...

"Grandma, grandma, LOOK!" said Li. "My tooth went WIBBLE WOBBLE WIBBLE WOBBLE WIBBLE WOBBLE and OUT!"
"Well, well, well," smiled Grandma. "I know just what to do!" she whispered. "Throw it up onto a neighbour's roof and make a big wish."
"OK," shouted Li and...

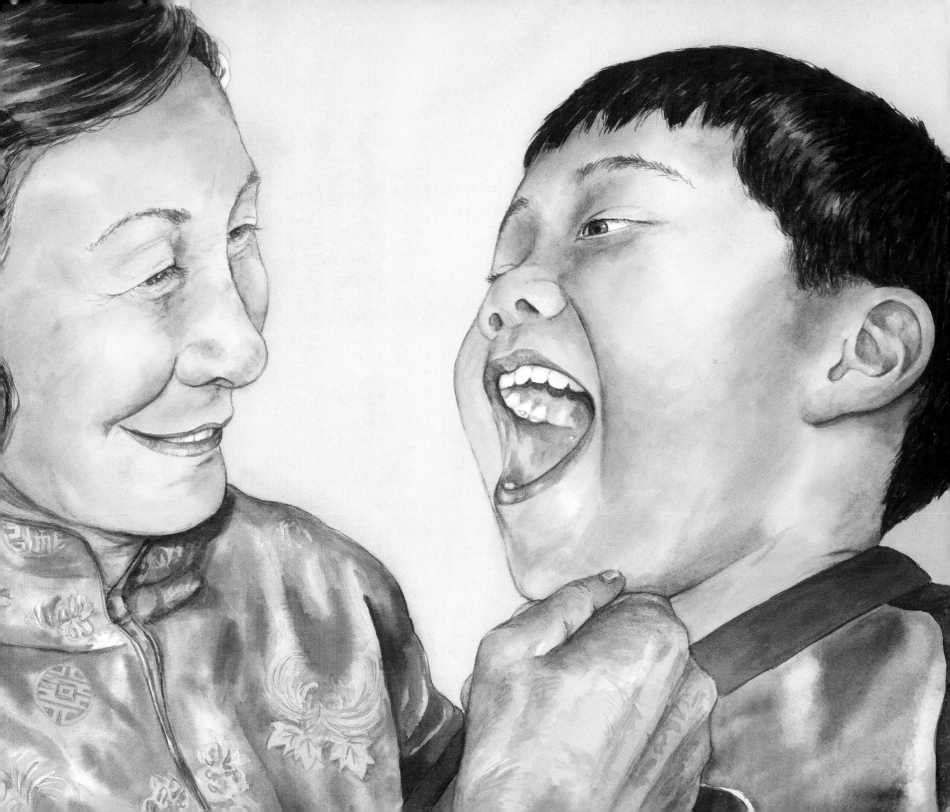

...und warf den Zahn hoch so weit er nur konnte!

...threw his tooth up with all his might!

Der nächste Tag war ein
Sonntag, aber nichts geschah.

The next day was Sunday
and nothing happened.

Aber am darauffolgenden Sonntagmorgen, um zwei Minuten nach sieben, wurde Li's Wunsch wahr!

But the next Sunday morning at two minutes past seven, Li's wish came true!

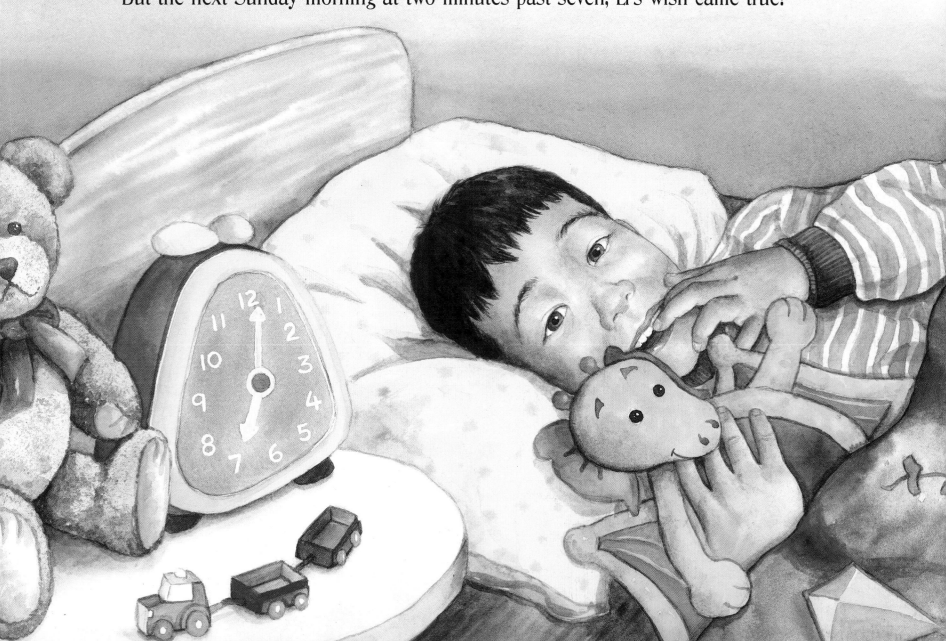

"Mama, Papa," flüsterte Li. "Guckt mal!"

"Mum, Dad," whispered Li. "Look!"

TOOTHY QUESTIONS

1. Have you lost your first tooth yet?

2. What do we need our teeth for?

3. How do you take care of your teeth?

4. When did you last visit the dentist?

5. Which one of these is best for taking care of teeth?
   a. Eating chocolate
   b. Brushing your teeth twice a day
   c. Climbing a tree

6. In some parts of the world people use different things to clean their teeth. Can you guess which they use?
   a. Apples
   b. Tea leaves
   c. Twigs

7. Which of these animals have the biggest teeth?
   a. Rats
   b. Wolves
   c. Elephants

TOOTHY ANSWERS

2. We need our teeth for eating and talking. They also make us look good when we smile!

5. Brushing your teeth twice a day.

6. Twigs from the Neem tree which grows in South Asia. They fight bacteria, protecting both the teeth and gums. The Neem tree is well known for its medicinal uses.

7. Elephants. Did you know that the tusks of an African elephant can grow up to 3.5 meters!